To Jane —

With love &
deep appreciation
for all your many
kindnesses and
constant
availability during
your Regional
years!

Rue.

6/10/07

Carried on the Wind

Carried on the Wind

Corona Ahrens

Covenanters

Published by
Covenanters Press
an imprint of
Zeticula
57 St Vincent Crescent
Glasgow
G3 8NQ
Scotland.

http://www.covenanters.co.uk
admin@covenanters.co.uk

Second (revised) edition 2007.

First published as *Borne on the Wind*, 1981
by T. Shand Publications

ISBN-13 978-1-905022-30-4 Paperback
ISBN-10   1 905022 30 1 Paperback

Dedicated
to the memory of my father,
Albert Edward Ahrens.

Contents

Preface

The majority of the poems contained in this revised edition of *Borne on the Wind* (now titled *Carried on the Wind*), have been known to me since their first published appearance in the early nineteen-eighties (the author being my 'Aunt Clemmy'). What I didn't notice then was that their central focus is in accord with a deeply held Franciscan practice - the practice of relationship. The stereotypical picture of Francis is a figure surrounded by living creatures with whom he is conversing, or relating, while he simultaneously rejoices in the natural elements of his environment. Francis was a man who was very much alive to his world and did not shut himself off from its ways - his celebrated relationship with Clare, for example, tells us that. Francis was no recluse but was yet a true contemplative. The poems in this new edition reflect this multi-layered nature of Francis who knew the depths and heights of the human experience, who gazed at life and found both delight and struggle in it.

The author of this collection has been a Franciscan Missionary of the Divine Motherhood for over fifty years. Many of these poems were penned when she was a younger self, during years of service in Africa and Gibraltar. What they reflect is a living heart constantly aware of its relationship to its central source, its founding narrative, its focus, which for Corona Ahrens, is her God. It was this God whom in her longest poem 'Vocation' she speaks of as enticing and wooing her towards the acceptance of a particular path. The image of her personal God is distinctly male, and the speaker in her poems is often female, thus an overt lover-like relationship is frequently created.

This may surprise anyone who has only a notional understanding of chosen celibacy but will be familiar to anyone acquainted with the writings of the mystics from time immemorial. What we need remember is that the writer in question here may have found her home within a religious congregation, but her heart has always been that of a living flesh and blood woman who, like any other, begins all relationships from that state of being. The blessed joys, the perplexing griefs, the silences, the questions, the answers involved in any sustained relationship are not avoided in Corona Ahrens' poetry but laid out on the page for us to recognise.

Both healthy and troubled relationships are found in the poems. The poem 'Magdalene', for example, is a deeply sensitive view on the untenable position of the trapped woman who has known only the shallowest of relationships. Described as 'a discarded toy, a used pawn' this damaged woman, for the first time in her life, experiences compassion. In 'Joseph and Mary' the focus is on Joseph and his almost impossible task of showing complete faith in his chosen partner, young mysteriously pregnant bride-to-be. This is a task of real love where there is 'a silent crumbling of all the human things/ the heart has planned'. Similar blind faith is present in the poem 'Mary's song to her unborn child' where the young mother already knows something of the searing loss that will face her in the future and yet is willing 'to bring you forth and give you to the waiting world'. This is a world which, in the poem 'The First Mass' crucifies her son and Mary 'goes back to memories of happier days/ As folk often will / When present pain / Is past all bearing.' These illustrations of turbulent and deeply painful relationships are balanced by poems such as

'The Waiting Time' and 'Bring me Home'where the speaker experiences her beloved's heart 'beating out my name' and knows the joy of surrender.

No writing of course lives in isolation and there are many literary and spiritual echoes to be heard in these poems. In the repeated draw on natural imagery I hear the voice of Gerard Manley Hopkins, Francis and Columba. In the fascination and struggles with the concept of Divine love I hear John Donne and Augustine. In the quiet acceptance of duty and the God of the everyday, I hear Julian of Norwich. In the settings and characters of various poems I hear the gospels. Above all I hear the voice of a single soul who is singing a poetical credo of all that has mattered to her. In this, the author's Golden Jubilee year, it is a beautiful lyric and a testament to a life lived deeply and lived well.

Anne McManus Scriven
2007

Introduction

All but one of this small clutch of poems came to birth during the almost sixteen years I spent living in a remote bush area of Zambia - 'The Waiting Time' is the exception as it was written in the 1970s in Gibraltar.

In Kasaba Mission, which was situated on the edge of a swampy lagoon running off Lake Banguelo – the smallest of the five great lakes of Africa - we were never idle for we ran a doctorless hospital, a leprosarium, a large out-patients clinic and innumerable out-stations. This was in the 1950/60s. there was no access to any form of the media such as one would have today: radio, tapes, compact discs, newspapers, television, telephone or wireless grid. Our mail usually came once a fortnight to a village seventeen miles away. I say 'usually' because we were never surprised when it didn't arrive. Thus we experienced all that is inherent in a life cut off from the outside world - its advantages (and they were many) and its disadvantages.

Woven into that sort of life and forming its background there is, inevitably, a loneliness which offers a choice. You either learn to live fruitfully with it or you allow it to erode your soul. I chose the former and, as a consequence, made the effort to find ways to become well read. On my occasional shopping trips to the 'outside world' I would beg, borrow – I never quite stole - some soul-sustaining reading matter: John of the Cross; the anonymously authored *The Cloud of Unknowing;* de Caussade's classics; Garrigou-Lagrange; Dom Marmion; Teresa of Avila, and others of that ilk. These, together with the biblical scriptures, taught me to 'go inside myself' where God dwelt and where I found resources I had not known were there.

It is perhaps strange but at that time I, a Franciscan, felt no attraction to Franciscan writings. Perhaps this was because some of the earlier translations were, to my mind, dull, lifeless and heavy with platitudes. It was only in the proliferation of Franciscan material and workshops which followed the Second Vatican Council that all that changed for me.

Sometimes, whilst in Kasaba going about my duties as nurse, midwife and general factotum, I would find thoughts running through my mind. These reflective thoughts would link themselves together in couplets or simple stray lines. I loved these thoughts and found comfort in them. One day, whilst in one of the villages vaccinating children against smallpox, one after the other after the other after the other in a never ending line of tired mothers struggling to hold crying children, we sat down to take a short break as we had been at it for hours. The mothers sat too and the children quietened down, now that we, their tormentors, had stopped attacking them. Except for the heat and the flies, all was more or less calm. It was whilst sitting there and thinking my own thoughts, that I decided that later I would write down the reflections which had, for some time, been playing quietly somewhere deep inside my mind. It was thus that these few poems came to be written.

When I left Africa I thought my heart would never recover. But it did, especially when later I was assigned to Jordan. By that time I had moved from nursing to teaching, and, in the Franciscan College in Amman, I spent nine years taking classes of thirty to thirty-five teenage Jordanian boys, all packed into one hot classroom, preparing them for their '0' levels. They were wonderful lads with a huge sense of fun which sometimes caused them to lead me a pretty dance, but there was never any malice in them. Like most teenagers they were mad on disco music and from them I learnt as much as I ever want to know about this genre, for they all belonged to some band or other and would thrust their cassettes on me with a plea to listen because 'You'll love it Sister, you really will.' So listen I did, love it I did not, but, because I loved them, I told them it was all 'great stuff'.

My mind often strays back to Jordan where, in spite of all the troubles, tensions and unrest of the Middle East, I lived happily and safely. I treasure my Jordanian memories: the evenings spent with friends, sitting on their patios overlooking the brown hills and experiencing the fullness of Arab hospitality; the evening drives we sometimes took out into the desert where, with no artificial light to block one's view, the velvet sky embedded with a million stars seemed near enough to touch. Surely this was the sight that inspired the psalmist to sing out in rapture:

When I see the heavens, the work of your hands,
the moon and the stars which you arranged -
What are we that you keep us in mind,
mortal beings that you care for us?

There was a poet if ever there was one. No human emotion is excluded from their outpouring to their God.

And what of the flowers? The Jordanian spring is very short but once it comes the word goes round: 'don't forget to go and see the flowers'. They only last a few days so if you miss them, you miss them. During that time the towns empty out in the evenings as the people drive out to see the desert in bloom; to witness nature gone wanton and in her prodigality spreading flowers everywhere. The dry expanses of dust yesterday are today covered with a carpet of blue, red and golden flowers.

And on a more mundane level, how I loved rooting around the Suuq bartering for what I wanted. What a game all that was, and how both buyer and seller enjoyed it.

After Jordan I returned to England and for four years was in London working with small children who, because English was their second or even third language, were lagging behind in class. I enjoyed my sessions with these young scholars all so painfully eager to learn. Towards the end of the lesson we would exchange roles and I would become the reader and the child the avid listener as I took him or her on a journey to the river bank where we met up with 'Mole' and 'Ratty'. I would sometimes try to introduce a different story but all to no avail, they all loved the enchantment of the small animals of the river bank. One day Leon, a little Ethiopian boy, told me that the previous night he had dreamt that he was helping Mole to whitewash his house. I felt a prick of tears for a few weeks previously all this child could speak of in his broken English were guns, tanks and soldiers. Were these now beginning to move out from his memory?

But Africa has the greatest pull on my memory – the Africa I knew, where we never needed to lock doors and could go walk-about in the villages any time of the day or night, happy in the company of people who were our neighbours and friends, our only fear being of snakes.

All this was a long time ago but I have not changed much. I no longer live in far away, inaccessible places – (though when the telephone or doorbell jangle too noisily I rather wish I did) – but I am now at home living in 'Ladywell', our congregational motherhouse in the heart of the Surrey countryside. I no longer write poetry though I still love to handle words, feeling the texture of them as I move them around this way and that to find where they fit comfortably with each other. This is one of the joys of my main task - which gives me the rather grandiose name of 'historian' but all that means is that I am engaged in researching and putting into readable form the rather complicated history of our congregation.

Ladywell is a very busy house but it has not quelled my need for quietness and solitude. One need not be on the edge of an African swamp with all its primeval beauty, or in the Jordanian desert looking at stars, or in a junior school in London seeing pools of innocence and delight in the eyes of small, rather confused, children as they allow their imagination to take them along the river bank visiting their animal friends, to appreciate how we all, including children, need some solitude, some dream time, in our lives. Time and place are always at one's elbow and always available if the heart's yearning is strong enough – waiting for a bus, travelling in a train, ironing one's clothes, taking a walk, sewing, and yes, even sitting in the dentist's waiting room, God is so near, just waiting to welcome us. What is to stop one?

I am sometimes asked why I no longer write poetry and the answer is simple: there is no urge to do so. Reflective poetry must start with something inside wanting to grow, wanting to be born and giving no rest until one brings it forth. That 'something' is not there so all I would write would be a doggerel. Maybe it will come again but until it does I content myself with my present tasks – writing, composing pieces of music for the community's use, playing the organ (sometimes well, sometimes not so well, but then my community is very tolerant).

My hope for these few poems is that those who dip into them will find something with which to resonate; something that will have meaning for them as they continue their own journey of faith. Might some even be encouraged to put their own thoughts and reflections onto paper?

My niece, Anne McManus Scriven, floated, and then took through, the idea of this revision and reprint. Sr. Ann Kiely, the then Congregational Leader of our FMDM congregation, gave the project her enthusiastic endorsement. With love I thank them both.

Corona Ahrens.
August 2007.

In my heart I found a seed,
and then another, until there
were many. All waiting.
I held them up on the open palm of
my hand that they might be carried
on the wind to others.
For the essence of gift is to share.

Vocation

It was in the Spring when you first spoke to me
I remember so well
for the warming days
and lengthening evenings
had paved calm avenues in my mind.
Areas of awareness,
where one who spoke in whisperings
could be heard.
You spoke to me of life and purpose
and I read your meaning
in the calm
steady
downward
beat of wing
of a homing mother-bird.
But...
I was young and very gay
and had filled my world
with love and laughter
friends and play
and felt no need to change my way.
I made to tell you so.
But somewhere in the twilight of my non-acceptance
you had already turned away.

For many months you did not come again
and I was glad to have it so
though that visit stayed memoried in my mind.
You had scattered seed,
and silently, in hidden lonely places.
Deep within me
it grounded
and began to grow.

When Spring gave place to Summer
I, though quite devoid of all intent,
would wait for you.
You, whom I did not know
and could not even name.
I waited you in all the warmth and promise that the
Summer brings:
sunsets,
dappled skies,
swallows' wings.
I waited you in all those tranquilities of time:
before dawn,
after rain,
the held goblet of wine.
I waited you in music and its power over me:
the raised baton
the first violins
the finished symphony.

Yet...
'neath it all there pulsed a steady ache
held in fixed intensity by a thread of knowledge
maturing into ripeness of pain.
Pain. For I began to know
that it was you who were making such inroads in my
life.
That you were planning plans and dreaming dreams
even as I had done,
And growing in the knowledge
my mind closed slowly in quiet dread,
chilled with cold,
and could not be warmed
with Summer sun.
Autumn came with all its homely claims,
and I watched the fullness of the forest trees

being shaped anew
in stark aesthetic lines
that somehow
spoke insistently
of you.
I tried to misread your message
in the slow browning of leaves
as they shed the glory of Summer sheen.
But instead I think I died a little
as I watched the Summer fade
and remembered all that it
and I had been.

Then...
in quiet desperation
I threw my final bid.
I set to build a wall
of every subterfuge I knew.
You waited courteously
until the work was almost done,
then, with divine nonchalance,
you tumbled every stone
and walked through.

Weariness has a force all its own
causing a seeming surrender
in which a whole world
of untapped strength
is kegged.
It brought me to decision.
A decision my whole being craved to reject.
Born of defeat. And yet once made
was iced into solidity
by Winter's piercing cold,
lifted high by strong winds

and set in course.
And thus the journey I had long postponed
began out among the stars.
And I saw the path quite clearly:
it was paved with gold.

And...
so it is that even now
when the dimmed perspective dulls my life
and grey routine logs my will,
when my feet weary
from trudging out a road
you have not asked me to traverse,
I remember the wooing days.
I remember
how you sought me,
questing me,
until you brought me
into your outflung arms
which caught me
holding me tightly,
lover-like,
above a storming sea of fears.

Yes...
I remember.
And in remembering
know a swell of tears
springing from the knowledge
of all that you have been
to my unresponding heart
down through the years.
But...
grace never brings an end
only new beginnings.

There is grace in all these tears,
they are not a wasted thing,
but the soft nurturing rain
of a second Spring.

I know this is so,
for all at once I hear your voice again:

in dappled skies,

sunsets,

the slow fall of rain.

I see your hand in those tranquilities of time:

before dawn,

on rippled seas,

the raised chalice of wine.

I know your love in every single thing:

the ray of sun

the leafless tree

the warmth and promise that only you can bring.

And...
In quietness and trust
I prepare my soul
whilst deep within me,
in the hidden trysting place,
it seems,
I hear you sing.

Sing Me a Song Mary

Sing me a song Mary
of water and waves
and breezes
blowing off tranquil seas.
Sing of joyousness and laughter,
and lights
which tease the leaves of swaying trees.
Sing of peace and happiness
of bird song
and the earth
carefully nurturing its seed.
My child, I sang all this long ago
one chill-filled dawn,
the day my babe - my Lord and yours -
was born.

A Christmas Poem

Mary, her mind a sheet of light
studded by a myriad thoughts
each a hushed star
rocked in the still deeps
of many waters.
Thoughts as yet unformed,
caressing,
soothing,
as gentle waves finger golden grains of sand
on vast deserted shores.
Her heart, joyed into singing
as soft winds sing
when moving through swaying corn
grown to full ripening.
Singing in sweet bewilderment
the song of her divine mothering.
Her soul, flighting in vast spirals
like birds over endless seas.
Soaring and drifting
yet plunging again
into the deep reaches of
unfathomed mystery.

Her will, given
absorbed in his
as wave and water are one.
Lost, as lesser lights are lost,
in the blaze of sun.
And I fall to thinking "What of me?

Dull driftwood, prey of every tide
on wild seas.
Have I no song to sing

to this swaddled sweetest thing
No proof of my caring?"

Then Mary smiles
and in her eyes I seem to see
dry and broken sea wood
burning itself in brightest blaze
before the babe
who draws its warmth
unknowingly.
And seeing this my mind folds silently
on my own inner peace
as on endless reaches of tranquil seas.
And I can think
no other thing.

The Magdalene

He looked at her
defiant in her sin
yet somehow beautiful.
For fear was there,
tempering her.
It lurked in the deep recesses of her angry eyes
and was caught, it seemed,
in the gleam of her burnished hair.

He watched her glance,
dark, despairing, thrown
at the tight knot of men
hard-cored in their fulfillment of the law.

He did not miss
the beautiful hands
opening and closing
clutching hopelessly
at futile straws.

And what is more he saw the child in her
who had reached out for love,
driven by need and loneliness.
He knew the woman in her
craving oneness
yet cheated in her search.

He felt the hopelessness of her now.
A discarded toy. A used pawn.
Condemned for her failure
to ride out the fury of the storm.
Anger and compassion twinned in him
and rose in a powerful spring.

There were depths there. He knew that.
Lying still and cool
beneath the turbulence of sin.

Love welled in him,
spilling over.
She was his to win.

"Cast the first stone", he cried out
"Whoever stands without guilt".
For he knew their hearts, their petty dealings,
their hidden sins and covered crimes.
He saw ungiven depths, calculating minds
shrunken into soured yellowness
by the relentless passage of time.
They turned to go
and pity replaced anger in him
They were so heavy in their tread.
And for a long space he stood silent
lost in his longing for them.

The woman quite forgotten
until a stir brought him round again
facing her instead.
She was calm now
anger and fear had lost their hold
and yet she was held still more
by a force unknown to her before.
For love was rising in her.
Tremulous at first,
yet thrilling in joyful newness
to the wonder of its own delayed birth.
Gaining as strong winds gain
when troubling darkened depths of seas
that roar beneath the pounding peaks
of foaming surf.

Aye, lust had lived its blackened night in her,
but death had been swift,
and all the ruined remnants
drowned in the eddying pools
of life new begun.

She rose and walked slowly away
over scorching sand
and was lost
in the blaze of sun.

Joseph and Mary

There was a lightness in her step as she left the well,
water pot held high,
and started off along the stony path
that echoed back to her with old familiar ring
as she chose her steps in order not to spill the
contents of her jar.
Joseph watched her from the heavy shade of the
cypress tree.
He had asked for her last night
and Joachim had agreed.
She was unaware of his presence
as she passed within a yard or two of where he stood
and yet her mind was filled with him.
Her soul reached out in song to him.
She knew him for the dear completion
of all the kept desires of her dawning womanhood.
"Know my love for you Joseph in the pulse of my
young blood.
Sound my joy in the depth of my given heart.
Hold my life as the womb cradles its little one
and I will give you all and keep no part.
Be to me as moon on crystal waters.
Shade of tree in harmful glare of sun
and I will be to you a soft and muted glowing
moving along the unfolding thoughts of your
cherished loves,
in all the unborn hours yet to come."
He watched her pass, and longed for her
as barren tree for leaf, lost sheep for fold.
He caught the gracious swing of her
as she moved in gentle stride
leaving prints in trodden dust - or
Was it gold that strewed the path behind her as she

went,
reflecting in its depths the limpid joy
of her yesterday's assent?

But...
Heaven, joy and blissful song
fluid hours and sunlit mind
are not for those whose lives have been touched
by the immensities of God's hand.
Life for them is rather a fleeting taste,
a stirred desire,
and then
a silent crumbling of all the human things
the heart has planned.
And so it was with Joseph, who, as time went on
began to know that all was not in keeping with the
law.
And as the knowledge grew in him
he tossed on waves of blackest night,
made blacker still by remembering
he joy that had gone before.
For she had been life and love to him,
moving in his being like soft winds
on summer plains.
Cresting and wooing the deeps in him
leaning his life in gentle folds
to the pressures of unknown claims.
She had been surging joy in him
enclosing his love in her warm earth
nourishing it to fullness of grain.
He knew no guilt of hers
was root of the new sprung life
that caused all his fears,
as painfully he travelled the farthest length of
privilege.

And the pain of it was this:
that in the darkness of his turmoiled depths
he knew she could never be his.
Despair ached its tortured way
down the fall of all the hours
that could not be lost in exhausted sleep.
Hours that caught the jagged edge of his broken
thoughts
and were shattered into mocking fragments of a love
he knew he could not keep.
But tears are not for men such as Joseph
only the pain they bear,
swollen into a thousand griefs,
telling of stretched out thoughts
and stark despair.
He groped amid the remnants of his strewn and
broken hopes,
seeking a wholeness
that in his saner mind
he knew
could not be there.
But all this was past now.
Hours had piled each other
and totalled to a count of years.
Time had soothed the stark point of pain
easing it to a place where it could be borne,
moulding it into his rebuilt life
where values could once again
be known as real.
And so, if at times Joseph walked alone
amid his memories and lost desires,
if in the course of starlit hours
he uncovered secret places in his mind
to handle again in gentlest hold
the thoughts and loves of earlier times,

none could tell.
For he had tuned the outer accent of his life
to humbler things
as a man caring for woman and child has need to do.
And those who looked on him could now comfortably
say
"With Joseph - all is well".

Mary's Song to her Unborn Child

Let me rock you dearest child,
gently,
as seas rock
in their deepest places.
Feel the pulse of my love
in the surging strength of my young blood.
And quieten. Quieten and wait.
As I also wait with you.
You are restless dearest child.
I feel your feet moving and anxious
eager for feel of sandal and turf.
Your head, tossing slightly
as small anchored boats toss,
straining for freedom and the buoyancy
of white-tipped surf.
I feel your small hands
groping, moving slowly
opening, learning to give.
And I know, as small mountain gorges know,
at the coming of first rains,
that my depths are only shallows,
and that you will spill over
and leave me drained.
But this is how it must be
for I feel moving within me,
immense peoples and nations
from the first to the last,
moving, surging, crying in the vastness
of their needs.
I feel endless waters
tiding onto unknown shores
searching, pleading but failing to find, and
returning again to the meaningless depths

of uncharted seas.
I must let you go dearest child
with my blood hot within you,
and your heart pulsed into being
by mine.
I will watch you, as the whole world
will take you from me.
And I will know
that this was all planned
before the coming of time.
But, for one more hour,
let me rock you
as seas rock in their deepest places.
Let me thrill to the pulsing of my blood
surging my life and love into you.
And then,
I will bring you forth and give you to the waiting
world.
And into my emptied womb
I will take instead
all the lonely needs of your people.
And, just as I have done for you
I will do again:
rock them,
gently,
as seas rock,
until you are born once more
in them.

The First Mass

Open air.
Sweaty crowds,
High pitched women and raucous men.
Crying children who should not have been there.
Flies and stray dogs
incensed by the smell of blood.
And the midday sun
throwing everything into an intolerable glare.
A hilltop altar.
Noise and confusion.
No order, peace or tidy ritual.
Only heat, weariness, pain and dirt.
And for three -
paralysing thirst.
A soldier yawns, tosses a coin.
Two men hum a recent song.
A mother gathers up her child, preparing to go.
It is all taking far too long.
This is the first Mass
facing the people
(We need not think it is something new).
Two acolytes of unlikely kind
flank this priest as he prepares
the crimson wine.
Then holding aloft the paten says:
"Accept, O Heavenly Father, this spotless Host...
Pray that He will accept,
your sacrifice - and mine."
The people cough and fidget.
They take so casually
as mobs and crowds so often can,
the direst human suffering
met with in a fellow man.

They do not even see
that every spasmed muscle screams and pleads relief
as the sun slowly blackens the once white flesh,
the twisted root of Isaiah's prophesy.
Perhaps some among them know
that this chalice must be raised
above the world,
above this motley mob,
which dances wildly in a plunging sea of lights
before the barely focusing eyes
of a dying God.
And what of Mary?
She waits,
hollowed out and drained.
Her thoughts reeling and darting in violent bursts
of seething pain.
She sees him,
her own son,
between heaven and earth
hung
like a flightless bird,
strung
across a blazing sky.
She sees the ripple of fine muscle
fashioned for striding in sun and drenching rain,
but now
never to know sandal, wind or sea again.
She goes back to memories of happier days
as folk often will
when the present pain
is past all bearing.
She sees him, her small boy,
growing in grace and wisdom
as has since been written,
yet , for the present, content to play,

dangling a string for the lazy amusement
of a tabby kitten.
Remembering this her broken mind closes quietly,
dreadfully, excluding all light.
And somewhere within her, in the place where
thoughts are made,
a heavy door swings slowly shut.
And it is night.

The first Mass is drawing to a close
The heaving priest,
flicking tongue on broken lips,
clutches the thin straw of consciousness,
yet slumps a mangled mess
with arms tautened upright against the sky.
An onlooker smiles tolerantly,
and the age-long seconds
go slowly,
slowly by.
Then, it is all over.
All has been done.
"Go, the Mass is ended", the priest says,
And all gather up their belongings
and scramble off
like ants in the sun.
The first Mass has been said.

The Waiting Time

I lost you for a while
and I thought my heart would die.
Die, in stretches of frayed-out endings.
Die, from fruitless searchings
and sickness;
And, I longed for it,
I longed to die.
I lost you
And all of Heaven became a sham.
No stars, no moon.
No tumbling swallows.
No surfing oceans nor kindly rain
could speak a word to me
now that you had gone.
My emptied heart was closed to them,
For...
Everything that had once been whole
powdered and scattered
before the little black winds
that snaked around the
hidden corners of my stricken soul.
All that had once been bright
greyed and slunk away into narrow inky pools
buried beneath the blackness of the night.
And how I longed to die.
But then ...
you came back.
Quietly, and as soft as fur,
into my heart you crept
tiptoeing on the waters.
(Not the turbid waters of my dried up springs
but on the crystal oceans of your dear love for me.)
O the joy of it!

The limpid laugh of it!
Your feet, divine feet,
treading out the waves, gold-crusted and firm,
that sang as only waves can sing,
whose moon-packed depths cradle and caress
the dear and beauteous footprints
of the radiant king.
Yes,
you came back.
And all of love and peace and happiness
came too.
And my heart's full strain was broken
in the blissful joy of homing you.

And yet..
I know that in the drawn out lengths
of those poor, lonely days,
when that which I took for death,
was but a waiting time,
I learned to love you more.
Responding to my heart's dear necessity
of pleading your return,
I searched out ways to entice you back.
Ways I had not thought about before.

So ...
When again you withdraw from me
I will know it for a waiting time,
whilst in my soul
I will prepare sup for you
and all of comfort
at my poor hearth.
And I will know that waiting is a precious thing,
set into the heart as a tranquil sign,
to be held for deeper nurturing,

against the slow passing of time.

Yes ...
I lost you for a while
And I thought my heart would die.
But you returned to me,
tiptoeing, nay, striding, into my life
catching me up in your laughing arms,
cradling my head against your very heart.
And I heard my name pulsing in your blood.
Ah, my dear one,
for me,
what more of bliss can heaven contain
now that I have heard your heart
beating out my name?

Bring Me home

Lord,
bring me home.
For my feet simply do not know
the right way
to go.
I set to right,
they go to left.
O in your mercy,
bring me home.

Do not persuade nor cajole.
Give no promises
of rewards yet to come.
But against all my resistance
take me along the right path,
for only so shall I find home.

Having spoken thus I wait
lest my boldness
should meet with reproof
and my plea go unheard.

But then -
I hear a quiet footfall.
I know it is the Lord.
I see a loving face.
I utter not a word.
He smiles and calls my name,
and falling,
I adore.

Printed in the United Kingdom
by Lightning Source UK Ltd.
123041UK00003B/508-513/A